COMPLETE
MARRIAGE

COMPLETE MARRIAGE

COEQUAL HIERARCHY

RICK THOMAS

COMPLETE MARRIAGE:
Coequal Hierarchy

ISBN 978-1-966741-10-7

Rick Thomas

Edited by Sheron Wallace

Life Over Coffee
8595 Pelham Rd Ste 400 #406,
Greenville, SC 29615
LifeOverCoffee.com

Dedication

To the Bride and the Groom

"Therefore a man shall leave his father and mother
and hold fast to his wife, and the two shall become one
flesh." This mystery is profound, and I am saying that it
refers to Christ and the church.

(Ephesians 5:31-32)

For additional resources, visit
lifeovercoffee.com

Table of Contents

Preface

Every person has dual roles. I'm a son, brother, husband, father, business owner, church member, and Christian—to name a few. Multiple roles with different responsibilities permit me to express more of God to Him and others throughout my life. Marriage is one of those unique relationship roles in which a couple has the opportunity to express God more profoundly within their covenant, to their family, and to their community. Marriage is a beautiful picture of Christ and His church, but that picture was marred by sin. Our collective fallenness is why every Christian couple should have an all-hands-on-deck mentality. Fixing what was broken in the Garden of Eden and spreading the beauty of Christ through a redeemed and restored marriage requires spouses to maximize their multiple God-given roles as Christian, male, female, leader, follower, brother, sister, etc. The smart and humble couple realizes this opportunity before them, which is why they encourage and help each other to be all God intended them to be within their marriage covenant, including their respective roles and responsibilities. For example,

- A wife submits to her husband and she disciples him as her brother because of her coequal hierarchy.

- A husband leads his wife while humbly receiving care from his sister in Christ. He, too, recognizes the coequal hierarchy within their relationship.

Their reciprocality is transcendent, practical, emulating, transformative, and God-glorifying. In this book, I take on some of the most challenging aspects of a couple's coequal, reciprocal hierarchy. We talk about the one-flesh marriage the way Paul taught it in Ephesians. We discuss the vital orientation of the home, appropriately entering into the secret thoughts of your spouse, what sex is like for a wife, and the unfortunate reality for a few wives, euphemistically called the doormat wife. There is much more in this practical book for any couple who wants to mature as covenantal partners. You will be challenged at every turn. My prayer is that God will meet you at those turns with the favor that provides new thoughts and concepts or refreshed reminders of familiar truths. This book will give you the practical guidance that will help transform your marriage. It is also a manual that will assist you as you hope and help to others.

Rick

Introduction

The best marriages are those in which each partner's distinct uniqueness works in a beautiful symmetry that enhances the other's strengths while compensating for their spouse's weaknesses. The worst marriages are those in which partners do not know how to help each other become a mature picture of Christ and His church. Their strengths do not support the other spouse's weaknesses, while their unique weaknesses become annoying interruptions to their life partner.

Visual Discipleship

If you meet with me for counseling or any discipleship situation, you're probably going to walk away with a few rudimentary, stick-figure sketches on blank sheets of paper. A picture is worth a thousand words. For years, I have kept a stack of printer paper on my desk, which I used to sketch spiritual concepts. A few years ago, I bought a digital tablet to show the sketches on a screen in the office and afterward zip them up to send the PDF versions to my counselees. Jesus, the master illustrator, was accomplished in this method of teaching others. He used illustrations to take a person from the concrete and practical to the abstract and spiritual (Luke 12:27). Christ used real-life examples to communicate lofty, God-focused truths. He would draw in the sand (John 8:1-11) or point to the sky (Matthew 6:26) to make His Father's truth come alive in the minds of His hearers. He used hair, lilies, birds, and fig trees (Matthew 21:19).

The time spent with Jesus, a master teacher, was visually stimulating and spiritually refreshing. Because every discipleship opportunity provides more information than a person can retain, it is wise to take advantage of the eye and ear gates and give them some things to take home for further review. Your goal is for the information to pass from short-term to long-term memory, aiding them to remember what they heard. A short counseling session or life over coffee with a friend will not accomplish this good aim. You want them to look, think, process, meditate, understand, remember, apply, and share with a friend. Sometimes, I would transform the sketches into an infographic and place them on our website for the benefit of our community. The infographic in this chapter is from a counseling moment with a couple who came for help.

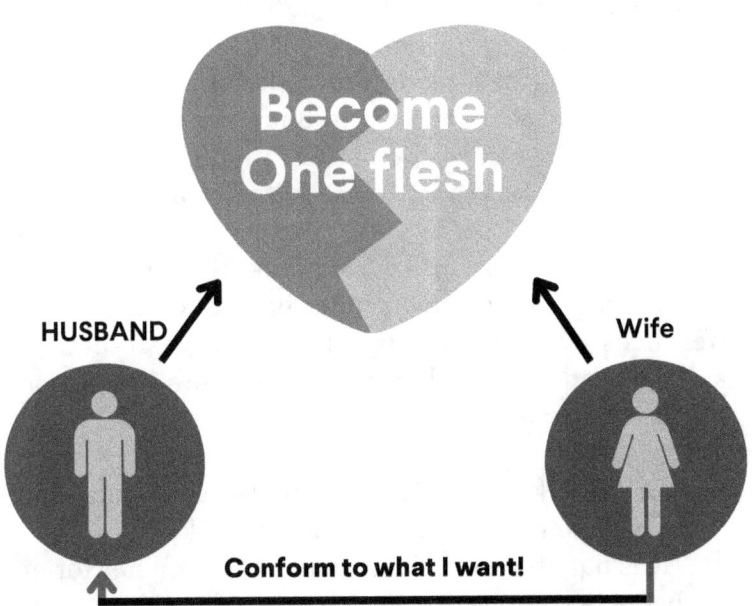

Breaking It Down

The divided heart at the top shows the problem and implied solution of marriage—one flesh. As you can see, there is division in their one-flesh union. The diagonal arrows demonstrate the direction each person in the partnership should go. Before their marriage, they were individuals, but after they tied the knot, they began a lifelong journey toward more in-depth one-flesh-ness. The long arrow at the bottom of the page—from right to left—illustrates how the husband expects his wife to adapt to his likes and preferences rather than leading her into the mysterious one-flesh relationship, allowing both their strengths and weaknesses to assimilate into the beauty of Christ and His church. (See Ephesians 5:25-33.) The problem with a marriage that does not emulate Christ and the church is typically, though not always, the husband's general attitude and practice that places pressure on his wife to conform to his wishes.

Of course, a wife can do similarly, especially if she has strengths that outshine her husband's. Being the leader does not mean he's more intelligent, mature, discerning, or further along in his relationship with Christ than his wife. Expecting your spouse to adapt to your strengths while ignoring your weaknesses rather than helping them mature according to how the Lord has gifted them will always create strife. Rather than seeing and leveraging the differences for something magnificent, a spouse may try to downgrade, ignore, or remove the differences while demanding the spouse assimilate to a marriage made in the dominating spouse's image. Here are a few examples:

- The wife likes organization, but it's not his gift. She demands that he become organized like her.
- He is punctual, but she is not. He rails on her for not being like him—on time.

- A spouse is social. The social spouse manipulates the other spouse to morph into a social extrovert, a person his reserved personality resists.

Strengths and Weaknesses

Knowing your spouse can do something better than you is a massive benefit to the marriage. Not recognizing their strengths or restricting your spouse from flexing their gifting can weaken and even kill a marriage. For example, a husband may choose to mask his weaknesses while draining the life out of her strengths. Alternatively, he could be transparent about where he fails while asking his wife to use her strengths to help him mature into ever-increasing Christlikeness. Adam was missing a rib, and Eve was the perfect person to make him whole. A key to marriage success is when two people are willing to humble themselves and have many conversations about their strengths and weaknesses. Their goal is to make the most of their strengths while transforming their weaknesses. These ideas became apparent to me years ago as I perceived Lucia's administrative gifting. She has the God-given gift of administration, which would make me a fool to drain that strength from her. Fanning the flame of her gifting has released me to use my strengths in other ways, which permits us to magnify God more profoundly than what either one of us could do individually. A key verse that makes a beautiful prayer along these lines is Psalm 34:3.

Oh, magnify the LORD with me, and let us exalt his name together.

Call to Action

1. What are a few of your spouse's strengths? How are you helping your spouse to use those strengths?
2. Do you struggle with your spouse's strengths? Have jealousy, competition, manipulation, anger, or other sins impinged upon the potential of your marriage? Please explain.
3. Assuming you do struggle, how is your spouse helping you to walk out repentance? What needs to happen for you to enter a deeper conversation about the possibility of this transformative opportunity in your marriage?
4. What are a few of your weaknesses? Are you allowing your spouse to enter into those weaknesses so your marriage can be stronger? If you're unable to talk at this depth, what needs to happen to benefit from this type of koinonia?

1

We Blew Up Our Marriage

Even with the best intentions and truest love, a marriage can go to some dangerous and dark places. Ours went there, which is why I decided the best thing we could do is blow up our marriage, reboot, and start over again, hoping to rebuild our covenant on a surer foundation. A caveat may appropriately modify the seeming hyperbole you just read. Lucia and I have always been best friends. From the moment we met on July 24, 1994, we clicked. There was hardly a time we didn't enjoy each other. Though we did have a few common interests, more things were uncommon between us, which I believe is vital for two people to maximize all that God would have them to be. Initially, our differences did not matter because of our desire to be together, even though some of them were starkly antithetical.

- I'm from the southern part of the United States. She's from the north.
- I was hardly in a church community as a child. She was always in a Christian community.
- I did big sinning. She stole a Lifesavers pack when she was seven.

- God saved me when I was twenty-five. God saved her when she was six.
- I did not care for my family. She had affection for her family.
- My childhood hardly had redemptive moments. Her childhood was replete with them.
- I liked wrestling. Lucia did not. Please pray for her.

Our Marriage Mission Statement

We want to become one flesh because it will allow us to reflect Christ more effectively than by being single. Therefore, we pray our marriage will:

Manifest the relationship of Christ and His Church to God, to each other, to our families and friends, and the world.

We pray our relationship will be a sweet offering to God, a blessing to each other, a testimony to our families and friends, and an opportunity to model Christianity to a world with no hope.

I could go on with our list of differences, but it did not matter. Lucia and I were buddies, partners, friends, and complementing lovers for life. Though we enjoyed each other, it was apparent early in our marriage something was missing. We loved God and each other, but our affection for each other began to wane. In the beginning, the little rubs turned into bigger rubs, with continuing and growing misunderstanding, miscommunication, and petty annoyances as we journeyed directionally the same way, but not necessarily conjoined. Most of the time, we ignored the big pink elephants in our marriage. As long as we pretended everything was okay, we continued to enjoy each other. It was like an unspoken "I'm okay; you're okay" agreement. Let's bury our collective heads in the sand and ignore the subtle and the overt. Sometimes, it was not possible to ignore everything. There was a low-grade frustration, and every few weeks, our not-so-easy-to-perceive anger would manifest as we vented on each other. We would not speak for a day or two as we gradually eased back into the marriage waters again.

It may help to reiterate that we loved each other. We were not enemies as much as ignorant, immature friends. Even though our Marriage Mission Statement had not changed and continued to be vital to us, we seemingly could not overcome this major broken koinonia hurdle. Neither one of us saw this kind of trouble coming when we were dating. For the first five years of our marriage, this negative vibe kept a low-grade churn just under the surface. Though hardly perceptible to others, there was a dynamic element missing in our lives. Layered on top of this problem was my job at our local church as the staff counselor. I was the fix-it person who helped people with weak, immature, or broken marriages. My vocation led to more personal perplexity and frustration as I served others with their problems but could not fix mine.

Then Came Jesus

At about the five-year mark in our marriage, we began to experience the gospel in a way that we had not previously understood or practiced. While we knew the gospel was for our salvation, we did not see it as a necessary solution for our sanctification. We both were discipled in a legalistic culture, which emphasized the rules while mostly ignoring the reason for the rules—Jesus Christ (the gospel). In one sense, we were a picture of what our Savior condemned in Matthew:

> Woe to you, scribes and Pharisees, hypocrites! For you are like whitewashed tombs, which outwardly appear beautiful, but within are full of dead people's bones and all uncleanness. So you also outwardly appear righteous to others, but within you are full of hypocrisy and lawlessness.
>
> (Matthew 23:27-28)

The difference between the folks the Savior was talking to and us is that we did love Him, and He had regenerated us. The real problem was that we did not know how to be authentically motivated by Him in our salvation experience or how to live for Him practically within our marriage. Our outward lives appeared to be okay—not in a hypocritical sense—but our dynamic, spiritual, animating, and internal lives were gospel-deficient. Behaviorally, we seemed to be okay, but our hearts were not in line with the practical gospel. We were hurting, and our frustrations spilled over into unkindness toward each other. It was a surreal, uncomfortable antithesis: we loved each other, but we were annoyed—at times—with each other, which led to dishonoring each other, a pesky little sin pattern that eats away at a covenant's koinonia's fabric.

> See to it that no one fails to obtain the grace of God; that no root of bitterness springs up and causes trouble, and by it many become defiled.
>
> (Hebrews 12:15)

Practicalizing the Gospel

As the gospel began to emerge in our sightlines, we gained clarity. The gospel—the person and work of Christ—motivated us to be more honest, more transparent, and more vulnerable with each other. A gospel-driven person knows they have nothing to prove, fear, or hide. We were worthless (Romans 3:12) before God found us, and what God gave us is a gift that we did not earn (1 Corinthians 4:7; Ephesians 2:8-9) and cannot lose (John 10:28). The gospel provides perfect love (John 3:16), which should cast out our fear and unnecessary inhibitions (1 John 4:18). We should be free to be honest and transparent with each other. Our problem was that we were not living in line with this gospel truth (Galatians 2:14). We did not want to be honest with each other, choosing not to let each other into our unspoken worlds where we harbored our frustrations and fears.

It was as though we were going to lose something if we opened up and talked to each other in a humble and vulnerable way. We did not understand the protective and persevering power of the gospel. The gospel frees us from striving. It releases us to trust God with our entire lives (Romans 8:31-39). It is true shalom and rest for the gospel-captured soul (Philippians 4:7). The gospel is God's power, but we were unwilling to submit our practical lives to it. We chose to rely on our unique plans and methods, which became vain attempts to fix our marriage. In time, it grew apparent God would not sit still for this. He began harassing me. Initially, I blamed Lucia for my internal soul noise and angst, but I knew the real truth about God's disturbing work in my soul. It was His high and holy love for me that motivated Him to stir the nest of my heart. His great love saved me, and it was His great love that would lead to a deeper sanctification. Paul captured these ideas nicely in 2 Corinthians chapters 1 and 12.

So, to keep me from being too proud...a thorn was given to me in the flesh...to harass me, to keep me from being too proud.

(2 Corinthians 12:7, personalized)

I had received the sentence of death. But that was to make me rely not on myself but on God who raises the dead.

(2 Corinthians 1:9, personalized)

God was saving me from myself. My primary problem was not with my wife but with God Himself. My Father wanted me to fix my relationship with Him first, and then He would help me begin repairing the relationship with my wife.

Tear Down That Wall

WARNING: I am not suggesting that you do what I am about to say, though it is what we did. This story is anecdotal, not a mandate for anyone to imitate or implement.

After the Lord had my attention, it was time to become a better leader in our marriage and address our mutually agreed-upon frustration. The plan of attack began with communication, so I called my church small group friend and asked him if he and his wife would be willing to take our children for a few hours. They were glad to do it. We dropped them off at their home and went to a local Krystal hamburger restaurant—a low-grade, fast food chain in America. If you don't know what a Krystal restaurant is, don't worry about it—you have not missed anything, and I have already warned you about emulating our plan. Krystal is about as low as you can go on the hamburger food chain, and this particular Krystal restaurant was beside a truck stop. It was the perfect place for us to begin rebuilding our relationship for several reasons.

- There were no children to distract us.
- There was no ambiance to draw our attention away from each other.
- There was no food worth praising.
- The smell of petroleum wafting through the restaurant was the perfect additive to keep us focused on the main thing—loving God and each other.

With all of the distractions removed from our lives, it was just Lucia and me sitting across from each other in a Krystal restaurant. We were about to have one of the more crucial talks of our marriage.

Humble Pie at Krystal

There we sat, looking vulnerable and a bit uncomfortable without our children. It was just us, staring at each other. It was the most challenging and humbling time of our marriage. It was the perfect time to put our Marriage Mission Statement to the test. I told Lucia that I did not know what to do regarding our marriage other than follow God's lead by having this meeting. I didn't know what to say. It all felt wooden and mechanical. We were going to places we had not been before. Then, I told Lucia that I did not like her and was not sure if I would ever like her the way that I knew I should. Though that might sound off-putting to some, I was literally saying the quiet part aloud. How many marriages do you know about who do not like each other but have not advanced the ball to this juncture of saying—in a redemptive manner—what they know to be true to each other? I told her that I was frustrated with her. I continued to share with her about my poor leadership and added that I was not sure if I wanted to lead her. These were not condemning statements as much as they were confessions. I was sharing with my wife where I was at the moment and where I had been for a while. I was sharing with her about how my weak relationship with God had plummeted and my faith was at a standstill.

Revealing the Log

You hypocrite, first take the log out of your own eye, and then you will see clearly to take the speck out of your brother's eye.

(Matthew 7:5)

In times past, I would share my disappointment but quickly blame her. It is the log/speak reversal. The gospel makes no allowance for this kind of foolishness. My wife's speck did not compare to my log. With this recalibrated gospel perspective—who is the biggest sinner in the room—it was easier to take the next step, which was forgiveness.

- Will you forgive me for my unkindness toward you?
- Will you forgive me for my harsh words toward you?
- Will you forgive me for my bitterness toward you?
- Will you forgive me for my lack of biblical leadership in our marriage?

Before, I was modeling a husband made in my image. I was not modeling a man created in the image of the Father's dear Son—the gospel. I look back on this now and think how I must have been out of my mind. I was. Sin is not being in your right mind—a gospel-centered mindset. It is a form of insanity. Paul would say,

Do nothing from selfish ambition or conceit, but in humility count others more significant than yourselves. Let each of you look not only to his own

interests, but also to the interests of others. Have this mind among yourselves, which is yours in Christ Jesus.

(Philippians 2:3-5)

I did not have the mind of Christ. For those of you who know Lucia, you can easily predict what happened next: She graciously forgave me. Then, she began confessing her sins against me. That's my wife. We both had murderous hearts (James 4:1-3). From where she was sitting, she could not see the log in my eye. The only log she saw was hers. She forgave me of my speck, and I forgave her of the speck in her eye. She continued to pursue personal humility while resisting any temptations toward pride. Rather than focusing on my sin, she asked me to forgive her for her unwillingness to complement the marriage effectively.

Serving Under the Cross

From there, we began a new marriage. We cleared the deck. God neutralized the sins in our lives. We could now talk about our relationships with God, how we needed to change, and how we could serve each other in the process of change. It is amazing what can happen in a relationship when God neutralizes the force of sin by the power of the gospel. It is amazing what can happen in a marriage when both spouses are willing to own their sins. For the record, we were not comfortable in our Krystal conversation. We were not gospel-centered professionals—by a long shot—and we're still not. At that table, at Krystal, we were nervous and imperfect, but we were determined to launch our boat in a different direction. Over the years, we have grown in our conversations about God and with each other. We have developed and borrowed many thoughts from many people who have helped us to keep the gospel at the center of our conversations. For example, here are some of our favorite questions that we ask each other. These queries are how we began to talk to each other back then, and how we continue to speak to each other today. I would love for you to read them and implement as many as you can as you engage your spouse.

Call to Action

A couple can measure their marriage by their willingness and ability to sit across from each other and ask these questions. This list is not exhaustive. One of your goals is to add to our list.

1. What is God doing in your life—practically speaking?
2. How is the grace of God working in a particular area of sin or weakness?
3. What specific areas are you still struggling with?
4. What have you read or listened to lately that is helping you in your sanctification? How is it helping?
5. Will you help me in this [particular area] of temptation in my life?
6. How can I serve you in a [particular area] of practical sanctification in your life?

2

His Needs – Her Needs

How do you know when a desire for love has changed into a need for love? It's an excellent question, and the first place to begin a diagnosis like this is with anger. Anger is the quickest way to discern if someone's craving for love has jumped from a desire to a controlling need. It is not necessarily wrong to desire something like love from another, but when a desire becomes all-controlling, we're in the deep weeds of relationship trouble. One of the ways you will know if your desire for something has taken over control of your mind is if you become sinfully angry when someone does not meet that desire. This concept applies to any desire you may have.

Desire Gone Bad

Let me illustrate how a desire goes bad by using this formulaic teaching from Paul Tripp:

1. **DESIRE:** "Will you do _____ for me?"
2. **NEED:** "You must do _____ for me."
3. **EXPECTATION:** "I'm now expecting you to do _____ for me."
4. **DISAPPOINTMENT:** "You didn't do _____ for me."

5. **PUNISHMENT:** "You didn't do _____ for me.
Therefore, I am going to make you pay."

Mable married Biff 21 years ago. Her desire is for him to love her according to her expectations. Mable's desire is sound, typical, and expected. She is not wrong. The problem is that Biff is a self-absorbed man. When they were dating, Biff did all the right things as far as demonstrating his love to her. She was convinced of his love and knew she had found the right guy. Unfortunately, Mable had a selfish, empty love cup modus operandi. When Biff brought her flowers, wrote her letters, and took her to fabulous dinners during their dating relationship, it all seemed right and precisely what she wanted. Biff had figured out her culturally conjured love languages. The subtle mis-calibration is that Mable was self-deceived. She had an undisclosed craving. Mable believed she needed and deserved a person who would give her a future according to her expectations—her desires. Mable lived in an idealistic and romanticized world of her making, coupled with a weak understanding of the doctrines of sin (hamartiology) and humanity (anthropology).

Mable was not spiritually prepared for real life, in a real marriage, with a real sinner. She was selfish and an idolater, which sounds harsh on the face of it, and it was a shock to her unperceptive soul. She masked the idolatry behind a normal desire for love. None of this was discernible because few people looked beyond the surface of their lives to ask the right questions about what was going on in their hearts. Biff selfishly conquered Mable, and she allowed him to capture her. And it all went well until Biff caught his prey and slowly turned to other things. After Biff bagged his wife, he was off to vocational pursuits and hobbies. Mable was left quietly craving while stewing over her losses. The truth is, Mable had redefined love as a need, and that is when things went very wrong in her heart. Note regression:

- **DESIRE:** Mable had a legitimate desire for love.
- **NEED:** Somewhere along the way, her desire for love morphed into a controlling need.
- **EXPECTATION:** Because she had redefined love from a desire to a need, there was an expectation placed on Biff's behavior.
- **DISAPPOINTMENT:** Though she did not know it, she set herself up for disappointment. No human, no matter how hard they try, is able to perform perfectly for another person. We're all sinners on our best day. Sadly, Biff was a jerk and never sought to love his wife like Christ. And Mable was more concerned about what she was not getting, motivating her to respond to Biff's sin with hers.
- **PUNISHMENT:** Her self-inflicted disappointment turned into retaliation. She punished Biff with her anger and other sins.

Both Biff and Mable were idolaters in their unique ways. Biff doesn't care for Mable, and Mable is hurt because she is not getting what she believes she deserves. The true need in their lives was mutual repentance, but they were not about to live out that kind of humility when we met at our first counseling session. They said they loved each other, but after spending a few minutes with them, it was apparent they did not. Biff loved Biff, and Mable loved her desire for love. They were bitter and angry at each other. The good news was that after 21 years of marriage, they decided it was time to get some help. In the midst of many bad decisions, going to counseling was one of the bright spots in their marriage.

Self-Defeating Complaining

Mable complained that Biff had not been meeting her needs, though she did not say it exactly that way. She said Biff was lazy, passive, non-romantic, selfish, harsh, critical, and angry. Mable also said that she was tired of being kind to him. Then, to punctuate her points, Mable shared over a dozen instances of Biff's selfishness. When she finished, Biff utterly sank into his seat with a white towel surrender look on his face. He seemed defeated, disinterested, and disheartened. I wondered to myself how much anger was simmering just below the surface of Biff's facade and how he had been punishing his wife all these years. Later in the counseling, I found out that he had been angry and disappointed in his wife for more than two decades.

Though Biff had been passive and lazy, and most of the other things Mable had mentioned, he added that her attitude also contributed to the problems in the marriage. He was right. Though he was not saying that to blame Mable for his sin, he was saying that her hostile attitude did not help matters. It's called a complicating factor to a pre-existing situation—added sins on top of the original problem. Isn't that the way it is with two people stuck in dysfunction? I've never met a couple, including Lucia and me, where one person was completely innocent while the other was utterly guilty. Just admitting this truth can have a massive impact on any marriage.

Who Fired First

With over two decades of marriage under their belts, no one knew how the dysfunction began. Truthfully, for counseling, it did not matter who fired the first shot. For Biff and Mable, blaming each other was the only thing that mattered. They seemed more interested in validating their positions and winning their arguments than seeing things from God's perspective. They spent most of their time attacking each other while affirming their rightness. That kind of "I'm-right-you're-wrong" sparring had nearly pushed God out of their marriage. Rather than spending time blaming each other, it would have been better if they had self-assessed their culpability in contributing to the marriage's dysfunction and then repented to God. Mable seemed to believe, by her words and actions, that if she repeatedly reminded Biff of all of his errors, he would change. Rarely is anyone motivated to change by nagging, complaining, or accusing. It indeed is not how the Savior approached us in our sin:

> Or do you presume on the riches of his kindness and forbearance and patience, not knowing that God's kindness is meant to lead you to repentance?
>
> (Romans 2:4)

> For by grace you have been saved through faith. And this is not your own doing; it is the gift of God.
>
> (Ephesians 2:8)

> But God shows his love for us in that while we were still sinners, Christ died for us.
>
> (Romans 5:8)

We could look into our past and find reasons to support why we are disappointed with others. Genuine Christian maturity is less interested in who did what wrong; instead, it is more interested in how to respond humbly to God and others. Biff and Mable were more interested in being right than being humble, and in the process, they grew more angry, bitter, and unforgiving.

A Sighting of Calvary

In time, Mable began to understand what she was doing to herself and her husband. She came to realize that while her desire for a great marriage was godly, her method for acquiring a godly marriage stunk. Quite simply, Mable forgot the gospel. She forgot how God brought her to

Himself. God did not bring Mable to Himself by being critical, harsh, angry, blaming, and unforgiving. The way the Father won the heart of Mable to Himself was through love, grace, mercy, kindness, patience, and, above all else, forgiveness. When Mable was reminded of the gospel during our counseling together, God mercifully turned on the light for her. Mable got it. She understood the gospel—or you could say that she re-understood the gospel. Rather than applying the gospel to her salvation, Mable began to apply it to her sanctification. Though the gospel affected her the day God saved her from her sins, she was starting to understand how to apply it to her everyday life, especially her marriage.

Mable realized that her husband could change and that she could be part of Biff's change process, but she first needed to change. She began to think about how God's kindness led to her repentance. Mable further realized how she was not modeling before her husband what the Savior had emulated for her (Romans 2:4). Mable began to address her sin issues. When she did, Mable was discouraged because she was unaware of how much she had been sinning against her husband. The more she went to God regarding her sin against her husband, the more she began to experience freedom from those sins that were previously controlling her. Mable also came to understand that what she wanted in her marriage was not an evil desire and that she should not give up on her desire. But she knew that she could not sin when she did not get what she wanted. Reflectively, she saw that her ongoing marriage problems compounded when she began to sin in response to her husband's sin. As she later said, "My desire was not wrong, but my attitude did stink."

Identifying the Ruling Motives

Mable blamed Biff for what she could not have. She accused him of withholding the thing she needed. The implication was that if Biff had acquiesced by giving Mable what she expected, she would have been happy. What she did not understand was that her desire for the relationship was not robbing her of her happiness. The loss Mable was experiencing was her idolatry. She was mad because Biff would not provide her idol. I asked her to repeat after me: "I would be happy if _____." My question to Mable was, "What would make you happy?" She quickly answered by saying that if Biff loved her the way she wanted to be loved, she would be happy. Her answer proved her idolatry.

The only right answer to "What is the primary thing that would make you happy?" is God. That was not the case for Mable, which is why she had an idol lodged in her heart. Whatever you believe you need to be happy is your functional god (God). If God's grace cannot overcome your lost expectations, your expectations are more significant than God's grace, and something has displaced the Lord from the center of your life. Mable repented to God and restored her relationship with Him. He became the centerpiece of her heart and mind, which played out in real, practical, and measurable ways. It was more than intellectual assent. The more Mable humbled herself before God through repentance and began to pursue Biff, the more Biff began to change. In time, their marriage turned into a godly relationship, and God granted her the desire of her heart.

DANGER, DANGER: Some spouses will read this and say, "I tried that" or "I've been doing that for years, and it has not worked." The primary goal is not to try something to get what you want. The main aim is to change for the glory of God regardless of any desired outcomes. I am profoundly sorry if your marriage is not what you want it to be. I have seen a thousand of these marriages. It is heartbreaking. Marriage dysfunction is part of the reason why I do what I do. I wish I could change your marriage, but I cannot change it any more than I can change mine. What I can do is change myself. My prayer for you is similar to the prayer of the three boys just before the king tossed them into the fire. They talked about how God may or may not deliver, but regardless of the fiery outcome, they would not submit to any idol.

> O Nebuchadnezzar, we have no need to answer you in this matter. If this be so, our God whom we serve is able to deliver us from the burning fiery furnace, and he will deliver us out of your hand, O king. But if not, be it known to you, O king, that we will not serve your gods or worship the golden image that you have set up.
>
> (Daniel 3:16-18)

Call to Action

1. What does your disappointment reveal about your heart?
2. Are you encouraged that the Lord would pinpoint an issue for you to change? If not, why not?
3. What if the Lord was using your marriage to sanctify you? How is it working; how are you changing? What do you need to do to find so much satisfaction in God that it drowns the sorrows of your marriage?

3

Follow the Leader

Every home has a leader. Someone must be in charge while everyone else follows the de-facto leader. I'm speaking of hierarchy in relationships, not the equality among fellow image-bearers. These concepts work together, not creating tension but fulfilling the possibilities of a God-centered home. As you think about your home, how would you define the orientation? Who is in charge? Who is the rightful person to take the reins of your family? Who do you want to lead?

Husband First

Biff is passionate about the Lord. Mable, Biff's wife, joyfully follows Biff. Bert, Bart, and Brice, the children, are humbly submitting to their parents. Benny and Biffina, the dog and cat, are fat, lazy, and happy. They are one big happy family like they ought to be. They have established the orientation of their home as God-centered. Their family is an excellent picture for us to use to evaluate our homes, making the husband's agenda straightforward: to follow hard after God. The Lord should be our passion, our goal, our life, and our leader. Let's suppose a husband loved God more than anything else in his life (Matthew 22:37). In that case, he is not only pointed in the right direction, but he has positioned himself to follow the leader while setting the right example to serve his family in the most useful way he possibly can (James 4:6-7).

If a husband is leaning heavily into God (Philippians 3:13), he will be sustained and equipped by God to emulate the leadership of God. If his wife is a Christian, she will more than likely follow him with joy. A woman would have to be insane not to desire a husband who is passionately in love with God, as evidenced by him practically being Jesus to her. Of course, part of his job description is to create an environment that compels his wife to follow him. He should be developing this kind of God-centered momentum in his home. If he is biblically crazy about God, his attitude, thoughts, and behaviors toward others will consistently transform him into the person and work of Jesus—the gospel. Even when he fails, his passion for God will motivate him to repent quickly, which will re-establish the God-centered orientation of his home.

Who's on Point?

Let's suppose that your wife is not following you. Before you begin to critique her, you may need to take a fresh and discerning look at yourself. Before you think about whom she is following, consider whom you are following, which implies the log, speck orientation (Matthew 7:3-5). Who is on point in your home? If the Lord is not the point person of your home, you need to change the leadership structure of your home (1 Corinthians 11:1). After a lot of living and a good bit of failing, one thing I have learned is that I cannot be trusted to be in charge of our home. My wife knows this, and so do our children. I have put my sin on display in our home many times (1 John 1:7-10). Hiding failures in a family is impossible. It is no secret to my family how I can mess things up. Lucia must know that I am not the leader of our family. She needs assurance. She needs to know there is someone more capable than me leading our home. As you evaluate your home, let these two ideas guide your thoughts and discussions:

- Who do you and your wife want to lead your family?
- Who does lead your family?

God Replacements

As you think about the orientation of your home, who or what would you say is on point? Who or what pulls your family along? What defines your home? Whoever or whatever is on the point of your family is your functional god (God). It could be the Lord, or it could be your work, ministry, activities, a spouse, or the children. Someone may ask how a person in ministry could not have God on the point of their family. My response is one of the sadder commentaries about the Christian community. It is no secret that the fallout rate among pastors is high, partly due to their inability (or unwillingness) to guide their families biblically. What's true for them is also true for the rest of us who lead small groups, Bible studies, and para-Church ministries but fail to lead our families. Ignoring family failure can be easy. Being ministry-minded more than marriage-minded is commonplace.

Some church leaders' ministries are a way of placing an ointment on the failures in the home. Many women in horrible marriages lead Bible studies. Being an example to their flock is not as important as filling a slot in the church or finding refuge from their home life, a brief moment of sanity in an otherwise disappointing family dynamic. If you are ignoring marriage and family failure while pursuing ministry activity, what keeps you from dealing with your marriage problems? Is it your reputation? Is it your craving for security? Is it your desire for approval? Is it not a priority of your church; are they more pragmatic than personal? Anything that replaces the work needed to put Christ on display in your life, marriage, and family is idolatry.

God replacements like these can suck the life out of what should be a vibrant, God-centered home. I have known many men in ministry who have undesirable marriages. Christians place these men on pedestals, praising them for their skills. Other husbands and dads spend their waking hours chasing the dollar. The American dream has duped them into pursuing the cultural lie of prosperity. They want the right neighborhood, the right job, a beautiful wife, activity-centered children, and the approval of their circle of friends. Too often, Christianity becomes a tack-on to their lives. Religion is a means to be connected to the right people while providing morality-based training for their children. Nominalism is a dangerous business. When God is not the point and purpose of these families, the fallout is inestimable.

Clogging the System

Have you ever sat in traffic behind a car that was not moving? All the other cars were moving, but you were in the only stopped line. The person in front of you was texting. That is what a wife feels like when her husband is not passionately pursuing God. He is preoccupied with other things. The Godward momentum of her family gridlocks because her husband is not progressing in his walk with the Lord. When the man is not moving forward, it hinders everyone behind him. In the movie, My Fair Lady, Eliza Doolittle was at the racetrack pulling for her favorite horse, Dover. Eliza was a lower-class Cockney flower girl who Henry Higgins was training in the ways of a proper lady. She was put to the test when asked to have tea at the track with some of the upper crust.

She did well until the race was closing in on the finish line, and her horse, Dover, was not moving fast enough. As the horses were heading toward the line, Eliza, in a momentary lapse into desperation, reached into her past and yelled, "Dover, move your blooming arse!" As you might imagine, all the proper ladies choked on their tea. They were flabbergasted. Though a Christian woman might not say it exactly the way Eliza did, that is how many of them think when their husbands are not leading in the sanctification of their home. It is as though the wife is running up her husband's backside because of his lack of spiritual forward movement. If your marriage and family are stagnating like this, here are a few questions for your consideration:

- Husband, does your wife humbly ask you to follow the Leader of your home?
- Do you have a hunger for God and a desire to follow Him as your family follows you? Do you know how to lead this way?
- Are you embarrassed to lead your family because you feel like a hypocrite?
- Wife, how are you encouraging and motivating your husband to lead you?
- Do you nag him? Are you critical of your husband?
- What is he more aware of, your critique and nagging or your encouragement and motivation?
- Can you and your spouse talk about the leadership failure in your home? If not, you must find help within your local church immediately.

Talking about Leadership

The first step in reorienting your home to God is to be able to speak about what is wrong with it. You will not be able to do this without the humbling power of the gospel working in both of your hearts. If you cannot talk about what has gone wrong in your marriage, you will need a gospel reorientation of the heart so you can have a gospel reorientation in your marriage and family. Only humble people can talk about what is wrong with them. Couples who cannot honestly and humbly share their faults and failures have drifted far from the truths proclaimed on Golgotha's hill. A man or woman who knows where they came from has nothing to prove, nothing to hide, and nothing to protect (1 Timothy 1:15). The gospelized person is not afraid of what others may know about them because they are resting in this truth:

> I was once a lost sinner, but now I am saved. I am the Lord's beloved child; His approval is all I need. By grace, God saved me. I do not fear what others think about me or what they may say about me. God has declared me free, not guilty, and pleasing to Him. The works of Christ define me. (See Romans 3:23; Ephesians 2:8–9; Mark 1:11; Hebrews 11:6; Proverbs 29:25.)

- What hinders you from talking about how each of you has failed the marriage?
- Husband, will you address your failures without attaching her failures to yours?
- Will you humbly ask your wife how you can lead her more effectively?
- Wife, will you address your failures without justifying or defending them?
- Will you humbly let your husband know how he can lead you more effectively?

The two most common misapplications regarding the orientation of the home concept are the child-centered home and the passive husband.

- **CHILD-CENTERED:** Some families put their children on point. Everything centers around them. The typical mom in a child-centered home can spend ten to fifteen years of her life in a minivan, caving to the culture's expectations for children, carting them around, and keeping them activity-centered. These children become increasingly self-centered as life revolves around what they want. They rarely learn humility, respect, or submission. They are typically weak when it comes to serving others; it was never their habit (Mark 10:45).

- **PASSIVE HUSBAND:** Another common problem in a family gone wrong is the spiritually passive male. The passive husband's home is where the wife takes on more of the spiritual leadership, while the man is preoccupied with other things that feed his self-centered preferences. The child-centered, passive-husband home is upside down. Typically, the child and the dad are in the same home since the lazy dad opens the door for the child to be the center of attention. Most parents don't realize the monster they are creating until the child becomes a teenager.

Call to Action

If your home's orientation focuses on the wrong person or things, please understand that you cannot correct what is wrong unless you both are willing to sit down, talk about it, and make a practical plan to change. If you will not talk about what's wrong, I appeal to you to find someone who can walk with you through these problems. The wrong orientation of the home rarely auto-corrects. If it continues, the future fallout will break your heart. There is only one right way for the home to function: the Lord must lead, and everyone else must practically follow His leadership.

1. Will you talk about the questions put forth in this chapter? Perhaps reading it again and highlighting the questions will benefit you.
2. Will you set aside time to talk about your marriage?
3. If not, will you find someone to help you and your spouse?
4. Are you in a church that values your marriage over your ministry? If not, you may need to seek help outside your church. You might need to find another church.
5. If only one of you is willing to make changes, will you begin making those changes today?

4

What Is Your Wife Thinking?

Most relationships begin with transparency, honesty, courage, and optimism. At some point, these things break down. The husband and wife drift from each other, and silence ensues. Even the best intentions derail if the couple does not know how to keep the transforming power of the gospel as the animating center of their relationship. Let me explain.

How They Meet

Boy meets girl. They begin to like each other. They soon figure out ways to spend time together. When they are not spending time together, they are strategizing how to spend time together. They become an item—a thing. They feel destiny in play. If the lovebirds are Christians, their thoughts are about sovereignty and providence: "God is in this!" It takes little effort to convince them how the good Lord meant them for each other. If they date for a year or less, there will probably be no major disagreements. If they date for a year or more, there will be a few ups and downs, but they will persevere through the rough spots—any thoughts of not getting married quickly evaporate. God forbid. A bird in the hand is better than whatever may be in the bushes. To start looking for another mate is harder than making a go with the one they have. They marry. From the time they met until their wedding day, they have become closer and closer, incrementally advancing in their call to becoming one flesh.

Each day reveals more about the other person, and what they learn about each other makes them mutually irresistible. This kind of bliss is how things ought to be. A one-flesh relationship is a never-ending journey. One-flesh-ness is a process of ever-increasing awareness and acceptance until death severs the love bond. Dating is what makes dating so exciting. It's the beginning of a unique relational adventure. Marriage enhances the journey as more of the mystery about the other person is made clear. Marriage is like walking into a garden maze full of beautiful flowers. Each turn reveals another variety, another aspect of the other person. The hidden becomes exposed. Even disappointment does not last because aroma of repentance gives them another chance that leads to more adventure and enchantment. Paul elevated this kind of Christ imagery in Ephesians 5:25–33, where he talked about the husband being a picture of Christ and the wife being a picture of His church. It is a high call with a great reward for any man or woman who wants a Christian marriage.

Ever-Increasing Distance

Then there is sin. Even in the best marriage stories, there is a darker side. The progression toward each other that they began during the dating season hits a few craggy rocks. Disappointment and discouragement begin to capture their optimistic hearts. For various reasons, the pursuit of symbiotic integration starts to lose speed. Instead of two people set on a course to incrementally engage and enjoy each other, they readjust, choosing to coexist rather than assimilate. It's the dual silo effect: twin towers standing side-by-side but never intersecting in a meaningful way. They become roommates or business partners. They coexist in parallel.

Earlier in their relationship, they could hardly wait to find out about each other. They talked freely and listened attentively. Now, the talking is selective, and the listening happens when it is convenient. They are mostly silent partners. Their communication is no longer an adventure. It is arduous. They learn more about what is going on with each other when they are with their friends. The husband listens as his wife shares her life with her girlfriend. He vicariously catches up on the latest happenings because he knows once they return home, catching up on her day turns to radio silence while the frustration that is between them continues to burn. How did this happen? How could two people who could not keep their hands off each other grow to a place where they have a lukewarm business relationship?

Weak Gospel

Unfortunately, few people go into a relationship with the gospel as the animating center of their lives. Without the gospel, no relationship can thrive or mature. People may coexist, but they will not grow in relational warmth. The force of the gospel is the working tandem of reconciliation and transformation. These things get lost in a deteriorating marriage. Christ came to die so we could be with Him forever. He entered our world and became like us. He lived a perfect life and gave Himself as a sacrifice for us. The Father accepted the work of the Son, which opened the door for reconciliation and transformation by Him. As Christ's followers, we can live out an echo of the gospel as we engage in our relationships. We cannot die for people to save them, but we can die to ourselves with the hope that God can use selfless sacrifices to help others change.

There is no relationship where it is more important to model this kind of gospel activity than in a marriage. Paul was not squeamish about this, nor did he hold back on how he thought about a man's responsibility in the marriage. Paul planted a man's marriage responsibilities right in the heart of the gospel (Ephesians 5:25). Christlike is how husbands are supposed to behave toward their wives. There is no wiggle room here. The gospel is more than a calling. It is an explanation—a definition—of how we are to engage our spouses. If a man marries a woman and does not have the gospel as the defining dynamic of his marriage, it will not be long before he spins out of his covenant, ready to give up on his promise. He may stay in the marriage, but his pursuit of his wife will diminish as the years drag on to some inevitable disappointing end. The vibrant life that was in the marriage will die, and the only thing that will sustain their union will be their mutual and agreed-upon responsibilities.

No Sin Plan

Without the gospel as the redemptive agent within a marriage, there will be no possibility to fend off the encroachments of sin. We have a gospel because there is sin. Without sin, there would be no need for the gospel. The conclusion is inevitable: a weakened gospel allows sin to breach the banks of marriage until the couple succumbs to its manipulations. The first sign of sin's advancement will happen within the first year of marriage. As an in love dating couple, they could not get enough of each other. As a mundane married couple, they will learn the rest of the story—the sinful side of their lives. The things they could hide or keep discreet while dating become front and center in the marriage. With a weakened gospel and no biblical plan to respond to the problems in their marriage, the partners become sitting ducks.

Every sin, whether small or large, slows their one-flesh momentum toward each other until they finally decide it's easier to coexist than to work through what is wrong. This fake-it-until-you-make-it worldview begins to shape their thoughts about marriage. It becomes the new standard. Silence sets in and takes over their lives. At first, it becomes small pockets of silence between them. With the angry couple left to themselves, these little pockets react like cancer does to the body. When the cancerous sin entered their marriage, they did not know how to take care of it. Like a stain on a carpet, they left it alone. After a while, there were more stains. They never perceived how such a small thing could metastasize into such a disease.

A Common Scenario

The most common scenario in which this happens is an angry husband. Few things will cause a wife to shut up and shut down like an angry man. The angry man is especially shocking if the new wife has not seen this dark side of her new husband. Even if she has seen it before, there is a monumental difference between dating an angry, harsh, and unkind man and marrying one. This scenario was Mable's initial surprise after she married Biff. Within the first six months of their marriage, Biff caught her off guard several times with his anger. Mable was a quick study. She learned when she should and should not approach Biff.

Mable learned to be silent. She learned not to speak her whole mind. Her quietness, albeit not her fault, was when the cancer in their marriage was activated. She used to be 100 percent involved in their mutually agreed-upon, reciprocal communication. After the first six months of marriage, she recoiled to about ninety-eight percent. Biff never discerned the subtle change because the slow incrementalization of silence was imperceptible. He was shocked beyond belief when she left him after thirty-two years of marriage. Only then did she give him her full mind. Mable was finally free to be Mable. After she had done her tour of duty with the children, she believed she deserved a break from her controlling and angry husband. Though she was not justified to leave him, she did it anyway. It was finished.

Do You Know?

Even Christian husbands are notorious for shutting down their wives while never perceiving they are doing it. They can be too dense, too stubborn, or too righteous to see or admit the adverse effect they have on their wives. It takes a lot of grace and humility for a man to take the lead by owning his role in the deterioration of his marriage. I have had wives come to counseling for the primary purpose of saying to their husbands what they were afraid to say to them at home. I have had scores of men tell me things they did not know about their wives until it was too late. She left, and after she was away from him, she began saying things she held in for years. Is there a cure for this? If this is your marriage, I appeal to you. It will take more humility and courage than you have probably ever needed to change the course of your marriage.

If you are willing to ask the Father for this kind of grace, you could begin laying the groundwork that could release your wife to be honest and transparent with you. It may take months for your wife to gain the courage to trust you, especially if you have used anger to keep her shut down and controlled. Even if you offer genuine repentance, she probably will not come out from hiding until she knows it is safe to do so, as evidenced by your practical and measurable transformation. If you are seeking this kind of corrective care in your marriage, you will need help. The hurts are too deep, and the memories are too fresh. You cannot know what you cannot know, and another set of eyes could serve you well. In addition to finding qualified help, you need to create an environment of grace for your wife to speak freely. When Lucia and I began making this kind of course correction in our marriage, I asked her if she would do this one thing:

> *Honey, if you knew you could say anything in the world to me and I would not respond in anger or with defensiveness or in any other way that would shut you down, what would you like to say to me?*

Of course, this had to be proven. Over the months, Lucia began to be more honest with me. She was initially timid because I had tempted her to fear. As she began trusting God and as I appropriated His grace into my life, she began to share things that she would only share with the Lord. In time, we renewed the adventure we began the first time we met. We chose to fall in love again. Rather than choosing the parallel paths of consenting roommates, we changed our marriage pathway. We were back on course, incrementally assimilating into each other.

Call the Action

1. Do you know what your wife is thinking? Please explain.
2. Are there pockets of silence in your relationship? If so, how did you get to this place?
3. Wife, are you motivating your husband to be open? Are you creating a context of grace for him to be free to speak with you? If not, what needs to change to be that person to him?
4. How vulnerable and transparent are you with each other? If you are not, why not?
5. If you are unwilling to work on a course correction, I appeal to you to reach out to your church's leadership. Let them inside your marriage. Do not put off getting help today.

5

Sex for a Woman

Sexual intimacy is one of the quickest indicators that reveals how a couple is doing in their marriage. Why? Because it is the most physical and intimate thing they will ever do together. It is different from talking, dating, dinner, or a movie. Sex requires more. Sex demands more from two people. You can do many things as a married couple and even pretend to get along, but sex is the litmus test that reveals the authentic reality of your covenant.

No Sex With Layers

It is not unusual for a couple to attend church together for thirty years and be miserable in their marriage. They can pretend in the public domain but not so much in the privacy of their bedroom. People can be faked out, but when it's time for physical intimacy, there is no faking. Though a wife may do her duty sex and the man may be oblivious, the fact is that the marriage is on hard times. Intimacy is either right, and their marriage is good, or it is not, and their marriage is in trouble. If their sexual life is disappointing, there is a reason: sin separates, and the bedroom is the most prominent place where they will discern this division. A good counseling question, when asked appropriately, is, "How is your sex life?" or "Talk to me about your sex life." Fortunately, the Bible speaks to everything (2 Peter 1:3-4), so we do not have to go elsewhere to figure out what is wrong with our marriages.

If we do not deal with sin biblically, the tectonic plates of our sex life will shift, and our marriages will be off-kilter. We will be out of harmony with each other, no matter what kind of front we present. Sin is what happened to our first sexual couple. Sin entered the picture, and division arrived. They felt shame, which motivated them to hide from the truth (Genesis 3:7). This one verse in Genesis explains eloquently, powerfully, and sadly why sex can be such a problem in marriage and why it is an indicator of the more profound issues a couple can experience. Sex is as transparent as two people can be, and if the marriage is not right, one or both partners will begin layering themselves with fig leaves. When sin enters, the fig leaves come on, people start hiding from each other, and there is no desire to be entirely vulnerable, exposed, open, transparent, or honest with the other person.

You cannot have real physical intimacy wearing layers of fig leaves. Suppose there is unresolved bitterness, anger, frustration, guilt, disrespect, unforgiveness, hurt, malice, or insensitivity in the marriage. In that case, one or both partners will be hesitant to become completely naked—vulnerable and transparent—to enjoy biblical sex thoroughly. No doubt a man can be mean to his wife and demand sex from her. I am also aware a woman can despise her husband and have sex with him. Hate or disrespect toward each other does not equate to biblical sex. Biblical sex is an uninhibited willingness to unite with another person in God-centered, other-centered, impassioned unity physically. God-centered sex is the most intimate picture of Christ and His church—thoroughly and comprehensively joined as husband and wife (Ephesians 5:28-30).

Starts with the Gospel

For the wife does not have authority over her own body, but the husband does. Likewise, the husband does not have authority over his own body, but the wife does.

(1 Corinthians 7:4)

Biblical sex is the height of physical/spiritual unity. Sin will not only alter this kind of intimacy, but it will reduce sex to a person's self-centered, self-satisfying, and self-serving cravings. Paul was able to bring the gospel to bear on all of life, which is why it is unsurprising that he had so much clarity on how the gospel should shape and form our minds when it comes to sex. The husband should give to his wife her conjugal rights, and likewise, the wife to her husband. You cannot read what Paul told the Corinthians without seeing the gospel orientation of what Paul was saying. The gospel—Jesus Christ—is all about going, giving, serving, and helping. Jesus was clear about His purpose and role on earth (Mark 10:45). He poured out His life as a ransom for others.

The word Christian means Christ-follower: we imitate Jesus (Ephesians 5:1; 1 Corinthians 11:1; Philippians 4:9). Imitating Christ is not rocket science. We follow Him in all things. When it comes to sex, we are to implement and fulfill the gospel's expectations. Sex is not mainly for or about me; it is primarily for my wife to enjoy. If she has a gospelized view on sex, she'll think similarly. The real question is whether I want to pollute the gospel by turning sexual love into a selfish pursuit. Porn is one of the worst manifestations of this kind of self-serving sex. Masturbation is another form of the me-centered sex worldview as the person satisfies him or herself.

Starts Outside the Bedroom

A poor sexual relationship is a symptom, not a cause. Though the symptom is inside the bedroom, the reason is outside. If you do not fix the real cause, your sexual experience with your spouse will never be right. Let me say it another way: If you are having sexual issues in the bedroom, sin is the culprit, and the first place you should look is outside your bedroom, where the sin is happening, specifically in the heart. Sex is an extension of who you are as a couple. If your intimacy is not right, there are things in your marriage that are not right. Your sexual life cannot be wrong, and that is the only thing wrong with you and your spouse.

Let me illustrate with a story that I trust is purely fictional for you. Suppose Biff slapped Mable across the face at 5 PM. It is now 10 PM, and Biff wants to have sex. Do you think Mable can freely give herself to Biff? Though I hope you have never slapped your wife, it is possible you could have done things that have caused her to put layers on, which has restricted your sexual experience. Some have said sex is a 24/7 experience for a wife and jokingly said it's about 5 minutes for a man. That is an ignorant and uninformed statement. Physical intimacy is a 24/7, lifetime experience between a man and a woman. To understand this, you must know what is involved for a woman to be genuinely free to give herself up to a man.

Working Without a Net

For a woman to be free to give herself up to a man, there must be conditions put in place. Let's think about this prospect for a moment. Let's begin with the typical sexual experience of a man on top of a woman. That can be a picture of what a biblical marriage should look like—a man leading and a woman following (submitting). For the woman to freely follow her husband, she needs assurance in two primary areas.

- Do you love me?
- Will you protect me? (Or, are you safe?)

Think about your most vulnerable moments in life where you sensed fear or the possibility of danger. What did you want to know from God?

- Dear Lord, do you love me?
- Dear Lord, will you protect me?

If you know God loves you, and you are aware of His protective care (Romans 8:31), you can be vulnerable and free to follow where He leads. God has your back (Genesis 39:2). Love and security are two of the most powerful things a man can provide for his wife to be free to love him well. Give her your love and protective care. God made Eve for Adam, not for Himself. Adam had a responsibility to take care of Eve, which he did by doing for her what God did for him: He loved her while providing a safe context for her to be vulnerable. If Eve sensed shame, guilt, harshness, frustration, disappointment, unkindness, or any other type of disapproving sin, she would have been reluctant to open up to Adam freely. Sin inhibits intimacy. Ultimately, this is what happened in Genesis 3:7.

Let's Go Farther

Think about what orgasm is like for a woman. (I know, I'm not a woman, but this is how I think about it.) Orgasm for a woman is a fantastical trip to a place where she loses momentary awareness of where she is as she enjoys the height of physical and spiritual delight. Let me illustrate. Have you ever played a game where you were blindfolded, and someone put a mystery food in your mouth? You would not play that game if you knew the other person did not love you and was not interested in protecting your well-being.

Similarly, a wife needs assurance that her husband is entirely in love with her and he only has her best interests at heart. He is her lover and protector. This kind of tested, practical assurance releases her to enjoy and experience lovemaking fully. If she is not confident of his loving and protective care, she will have one eye on him during sex and one eye on her desire to enjoy it. She will be torn (James 1:5-8). At best, it would be a double-minded sexual experience, which is a frustrating experience. She will not have assurances of his love because of how he has responded to her outside the bedroom. You cannot fake genuine love. If you love your wife, she will know it. That kind of love looks like the love of Christ, which frees your wife to close both eyes and take a fantastical, delightful trip with her husband.

The Love Of Christ

There are several templates that we find in God's Word to give us clarity on what the love of Christ looks like in marriage. 1 Corinthians 13:4-7 is one such template. Another one I like is what we call the fruit of the Spirit (Galatians 5:22-23). Galatians is the main template that I use to gauge how I think about and treat my wife. Nothing will remove the layers of reticence and send a wife into the freedom of intimate love like a man who is exhibiting these Christlike character traits. These nine questions are excellent for assessing your outside-the-bedroom love for your wife. I'm asking these in a closed-ended way, but if any of them apply to you, I appeal to you to open them up by thinking, reflecting, processing, and applying, which may mean having a conversation with your spouse.

- **LOVE:** Does your spouse see, experience, and feel your affectionate love?
- **JOY:** Is your spouse affected by the joy that you have in the Lord?

- **PEACE:** Is your spouse affected by the peace you have in your soul?
- **PATIENCE:** Is your spouse a regular recipient of your patience?
- **KINDNESS:** Would your spouse characterize your actions and reactions as kind?
- **GOODNESS:** Is your spouse a regular recipient of God's goodness through you?
- **FAITHFULNESS:** Does your spouse find security in your faithfulness?
- **GENTLENESS:** Is your spouse relaxed around you, and do they feel your gentle warmth?
- **SELF-CONTROL:** Does your spouse feel secure around you, knowing God is controlling you?

Practically Speaking

Imagine if your wife experienced this kind of love from you. The love of Christ coming through you would release her to be vulnerable with you. If you both are humble, I recommend you talk about this chapter (James 4:6). If one or both of you are not humble, I suggest you find help because there are unresolved problems that hinder you from reaching a place of maturity to have a Christian conversation about your sexual relationship. The critical thing to know is your wife must be free to be sexual with you, and if you are not treating her like God's treasure (1 Peter 3:7), your bedroom experience will always be less than what God intends. You cannot be snarky, mean, non-affirming, nasty, or unforgiving to your spouse and expect things to be right in the bedroom. You make things right outside the bedroom, and things will typically take care of themselves inside the bedroom. One of the most obvious but overlooked aspects of making things right outside the bedroom is a lack of daily repentance in the Christian home. Most Christians do not clean up their relational messes because they do not know how to repent. Active repentance is the only way God has given us to clean up our messes.

Call to Action

Dear Husband,

Be a leader. Lead your wife. If you want her to respect you, act like Jesus. If you do not imitate Jesus, humbly repent, remove the mistake, and begin emulating Jesus again. As God told Job, "Dress for action like a man" (Job 38:3). That means, "Pull up your britches and be a man." Give your wife something to respect. Take a hard look at the character of Christ, as seen in the fruit of the Spirit. Ask God to give you the grace to assess yourself soberly. Find a true friend who will help you change.

Unless your wife is unregenerate or insane, she will love you for it. Perchance she refuses to change, you can still be right with God. Be a God-centered, gospel-motivated, Christ-loving, Spirit-empowered, Bible-informed man for the glory of God regardless of how she responds to or treats you.

6

Respecting Unkind Husbands

One of the problems with some marriages is a lack of respect from the wife for the husband. A proper probing question follows: what does that mean? Is her lack of respect the entire problem in the marriage, or are there other complexities that might contribute to her lack of respect? There are always complexities in relational conflict, but why do some folks focus only on one track in a two-track marriage? It appears these eisogetes are extracting Paul's words about respecting the husband and missing the context. What if we take a look at the context and content of this pivotal passage about marriage?

> Wives, submit to your own husbands, as to the Lord. For the husband is the head of the wife even as Christ is the head of the church, his body, and is himself its Savior. Now as the church submits to Christ, so also wives should submit in everything to their husbands. Husbands, love your wives, as Christ loved the church and gave himself up for her, that he might sanctify her, having cleansed her by the washing of water with the word, so that he might present the church to himself in splendor,

without spot or wrinkle or any such thing, that she might be holy and without blemish. In the same way husbands should love their wives as their own bodies. He who loves his wife loves himself. For no one ever hated his own flesh, but nourishes and cherishes it, just as Christ does the church, because we are members of his body. "Therefore a man shall leave his father and mother and hold fast to his wife, and the two shall become one flesh." This mystery is profound, and I am saying that it refers to Christ and the church. However, let each one of you love his wife as himself, and let the wife see that she respects her husband.

(Ephesians 5:22-33)

Respect with Context

"She respects her husband" are the last four words in a section of Scripture where Paul is talking about Christ and the church while making a few application points for husbands and wives. These last four words are from a more fabulous body of thought, which begs the question, "When you read a letter from a friend, have you ever taken the last four words of that letter and developed a way of thinking that is divorced from the context of the letter?" Most people consider that to be an odd, if not a dangerous method of interpreting and applying a letter from a friend. The wise, prudent thing to do is to read the last four words of the passage in context with all the other words, not decoupling them from the main point the writer makes. Every Bible passage has one point, not two. Each author's intent is singular, not multiple. While we can make multiple applications from a passage, we can only have one point.

Of course, the applications cannot be disconnected from the point of the passage, or our application could alter the author's point. Changing the point of a passage is called eisegesis, where a person reads into the passage what he wants it to say rather than allowing the passage to speak for itself. This problem is why it's essential to understand Paul's point in what has been primarily considered a passage on marriage. Before I go into a fuller understanding of what those final four words mean, it would help to talk about what Paul intends with the whole passage. Nearly every time those four words are lopped off and lifted out of the passage, Paul's words become twisted into an odd application that he did not intend. Namely, the wife is supposed to respect her husband with no context, caveat, qualification, or elaboration. That is an embarrassing interpretation of the passage at best and damaging to wives and families at its worst. Mercifully, Paul did not leave us in doubt about what he meant because the meaning of the passage is right in the middle of it.

Point of the Passage

So that he might present the church to himself.
(Ephesians 5:27)

The point of this passage is about Christ and the church and what that means to us. Paul is elevating this mysterious idea of Christ and the church with a particular emphasis on the unity between the head (Christ) and the body (Church). Paul was abundantly clear about what he wanted to highlight in this passage. It is Christ and the church, not the husband and wife. The husband and wife in this specific passage are illustrations that point to his main idea—Christ and the church. Paul was careful and clear to make sure we saw the beauty and unity of Christ and the church. You see this at the heart of the Ephesians passage:

So that he might present the church to himself in
splendor, without spot or wrinkle or any such thing,
that she might be holy and without blemish.
(Ephesians 5:27)

His next words are, "In the same way, husbands should love their wives as their own bodies." He is making an application from his main point: Christ and the church, not the other way around. Paul is introducing a situation—marriage—that is similar to the point of the passage. He does not talk about the husband and wife and then says, "In the same way, this is how you should think about Christ and the church." That would make marriage the main point, and Christ and the church would illustrate the marriage point. To say the point of the passage is about husbands and wives, while Christ and the church are secondary, at best, is to read into it an agenda that Paul does not have. Each time he talks about marriage in this passage, he connects it to Christ and the church. You see that with his conjunction in the same way. Secondly, you see it when he talks about the mystery of the husband and wife relationship. He says the profundity of that mystery was to point to Christ and the church, which brings you back to the point of the passage.

"Therefore, a man shall leave his father and mother
and hold fast to his wife, and the two shall become
one flesh." This mystery is profound, and I am
saying that it refers to Christ and the church.
(Ephesians 5:31-32)

Chiastic Structure

A way to understand the point of the passage is to lay it out the way Paul wrote it. He used a standard literary device called a chiasm or a chiastic structure. Chiasmus had an essential place in Christianity. Chiasmus was very important in ancient texts, as it was a way to strike a balance in a work of literature. You may find examples of chiasmus in ancient Greek, Hebrew, and Latin texts and many religious scriptures. The word chiasmus starts with the Greek letter chi, also the letter that begins Christ's name. The X that makes this sound in Greek also looks like the cross upon which Christ was crucified. Therefore, chiasmus was important for Christian poets to represent Christ and His crucifixion. A chiasm is writing something and restating it (or a similar idea) in reverse order: ABBA. Thus, a chiasm looks like an X, hence the Greek letter chi. This standard literary device is not exclusive to the Bible, though you find this writing technique throughout the Bible. When you find a chiasmus in a place of literature, such as the works of John Milton in Paradise Lost, it is a very intentional way to add more religious significance to that line. Let me share with you five simple chiasmus.

- *"Ask not what your country can do for you. Ask what you can do for your country."*
  – John Kennedy
- *"One should eat to live, not live to eat."*
  – Cicero
- *"All for one and one for all."* – Motto of the Three Musketeers
- *"They take good care of their trucks because their trucks take good care of them."*
  – Advertising slogan for Dodge trucks.
- *"By failing to prepare, you are preparing to fail."*
  – Ben Franklin

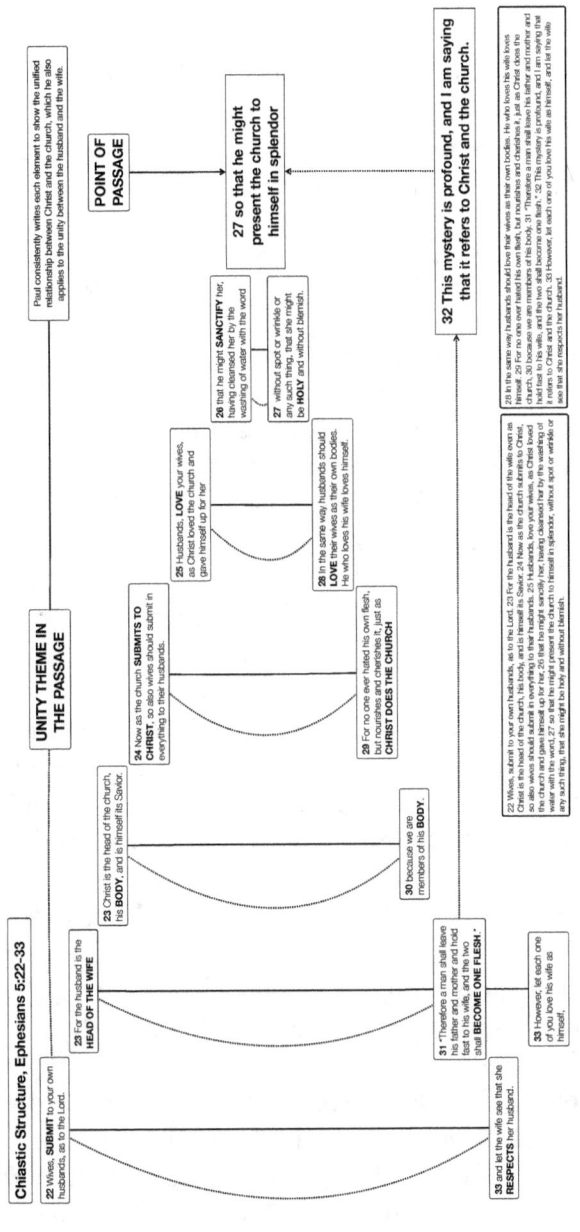

Chiastic Structure, Ephesians 5:22-33

UNITY THEME IN THE PASSAGE

Paul consistently writes each element to show the unified relationship between Christ and the church, which he also applies to the unity between the husband and the wife.

POINT OF PASSAGE

22 Wives, **SUBMIT** to your own husbands, as to the Lord.

23 For the husband is the **HEAD OF THE WIFE**

23 Christ is the head of the church, his **BODY**, and is himself its Savior.

24 Now as the church **SUBMITS TO CHRIST**, so also wives should submit in everything to their husbands.

25 Husbands, **LOVE** your wives, as Christ loved the church and gave himself up for her

26 that he might **SANCTIFY** her, having cleansed her by the washing of water with the word

27 without spot or wrinkle or any such thing, that she might be **HOLY** and without blemish.

27 so that he might present the church to himself in splendor

28 In the same way, husbands should **LOVE** their wives as their own bodies. He who loves his wife loves himself.

29 For no one ever hated his own flesh, but nourishes and cherishes it, just as **CHRIST DOES THE CHURCH**

30 because we are members of his **BODY**.

31 "Therefore a man shall leave his father and mother and hold fast to his wife, and the two shall **BECOME ONE FLESH**."

32 This mystery is profound, and I am saying that it refers to Christ and the church.

33 and let the wife see that she **RESPECTS** her husband.

33 However, let each one of you loves his wife as himself,

22 Wives, submit to your own husbands, as to the Lord. 23 For the husband is the head of the wife even as Christ is the head of the church, his body, and is himself its Savior. 24 Now as the church submits to Christ, so also wives should submit in everything to their husbands. 25 Husbands, love your wives, as Christ loved the church and gave himself up for her, 26 that he might sanctify her, having cleansed her by the washing of water with the word, 27 so that he might present the church to himself in splendor, without spot or wrinkle or any such thing, that she might be holy and without blemish.

28 In the same way husbands should love their wives as their own bodies. He who loves his wife loves himself. 29 For no one ever hated his own flesh, but nourishes and cherishes it, just as Christ does the church, 30 because we are members of his body. 31 "Therefore a man shall leave his father and mother and hold fast to his wife, and the two shall become one flesh." 32 This mystery is profound, and I am saying that it refers to Christ and the church. 33 However, let each one of you love his wife as himself, and let the wife see that she respects her husband.

In a more developed chiasm, the X (ABXBA) marks the centerpiece of the thought, which is the intentional, inserted emphasis of the chiasm—the main point, if you will—which is what we have in Paul's chiastic development of Ephesians 5:22-33. As you can see in the chiastic structure, X marks the spot: the intentional, inserted emphasis of the passage: "So that he might present the church to himself."

Theme of the Passage

With Christ and the church fixed as the point of the passage, the next most obvious thing is how Paul drives home a unity theme between Christ and the church. Paul consistently writes each element to show the harmonious relationship between Christ and the church, which he also applies to the unity between the husband and the wife. You cannot have one (Christ or the husband) without the other (church or the wife). They are not connected like they were contiguous, but they are part of each other. They are one flesh, not two. Of course, there is a discussion about leading and following, but that is not Paul's main idea in this paragraph. We must begin with unity before discussing roles. Each of the statements below makes a case for the unity of Christ, the church, and the husband and wife. Their roles flow out of their unity. Thus, here are nine common sense unity statements.

- Wives, submit to your own husbands, as to the Lord. v. 22
- For the husband is the head of the wife. v. 23
- Christ is the head of the church, his body, and is Himself its Savior. v. 23
- Now as the church submits to Christ, so also wives should submit in everything to their husbands. v. 24
- In the same way husbands should love their wives as their own bodies. He who loves his wife loves himself. v. 28

- For no one ever hated his own flesh, but nourishes and cherishes it, just as Christ does the church. v. 29
- Because we are members of His body. v. 30
- "Therefore a man shall leave his father and mother and hold fast to his wife, and the two shall become one flesh." v. 31
- However, let each one of you love his wife as himself, and let the wife see that she respects her husband. v. 33

Paul's unity statements are the only ways one flesh can function well. As the chiasm reflects, you cannot have one idea without the other. They are both essential to making a unified whole. For, if the wife submits to the husband, there must be a husband for her to submit to. If the husband is the head of the wife, there must be a wife for him to be the head of to function well. They are one. At every turn, you see the unification of two parts. They are one flesh, a mystery that points to Christ and the church.

Marriage, Practically Speaking

With Christ and the church as the point of the passage and unity as the theme, you're ready to address Paul's application points about leading and following, loving and respecting. The point of this chapter in this book is specifically about a wife respecting her husband. More pointedly, should she respect her unkind husband? As I stated at the beginning, the answer is an absolute yes; she should respect her husband. However, here is the problem. If you take those four words, lop them off, and lift them from the context of the passage, all you're going to do is rail at the wife for not respecting her husband without taking the time to address the reason(s) she is not respecting (or submitting).

- She may not respect her husband because she is not a Christian and, thus, rejects Christian teaching.
- She may not respect her husband because she

is a hard-line feminist who rejects anything that resembles Christian teaching, especially anything about respecting or submitting to a man.

- She may rebel against her husband because she has a sinful disposition to rebel.
- She may not respect her husband because he is harsh, unkind, and brutish, making it hard to respect or submit to him.
- She may want to respect him, but he makes it hard to do so. She's honestly trying, but he's not a good person.

The word respect means reverence for her husband. It is reverential fear similar to how we think about the fear of God. She is not afraid of her husband. To be frightened of him and to have reverential fear (respect) are two opposing concepts.

Examine the Whole Body

However, if the husband is harsh, unkind, or mean to her, she will be afraid of him. This common-sense truth is why it is essential to interpret Paul's passage correctly. It's about the unity between Christ and the church, which we should model similarly in marriage. Let me illustrate: If your calf muscle had a painful cramp, you could make a blanket mandate to your leg that it should not cramp up any longer. You could yell at your calf. You could say embarrassing, condemning, and other manipulating things to your leg to gaslight it into functioning as it should. Of course, you know that is ridiculous. Your leg is part of your body. You are a unified whole. Yes, no doubt, your leg should not have cramps. It should respect your body and cooperate with it.

But it would be best if you did all you could to ensure it does not have cramps. Manipulating your leg without careful analysis or addressing the whole body problem is ignorant and futile. In nearly every case, you'll find more things wrong in your body than just an isolated cramp. Why? Because no part of the body is uninfluenced by or un-influencing to the rest of the body. When it comes to Christ and the church, we know if there is a problem in the church, it's not with Christ because the head of the body is perfect in every way. But when it comes to marriage problems, like a disrespectful wife, it would be careless and harmful to think the husband has no role in their one flesh problem. Perhaps he is squeaky clean, and the lack of respect is all on the wife. Perhaps. However, to put the total blame on a disrespecting wife without a complete and honest examination of the unified body is misguided and misapplication of this passage.

Call to Action

1. Should your wife respect you? Of course, she should.
2. Does your wife respect you? Yes or no.
3. If she does not, how have you addressed the problem? Have you made it all about her lack of respect, or are you looking into a complete cure that factors in all the possibilities in the body, including you?
4. If your wife does not respect you, what is your comprehensive practical plan to bring resolution to this marriage problem?

7

Correcting Authoritarians

No human has absolute authority over another. This perspective should be common sense, but it's not for everyone, including Christians. A dictatorial husband and father can put wives and children in a difficult spot, which begs the question that folks have asked me for decades: "Do you think it's right to correct my authoritarian husband?" This chapter will be instructive and directive for those in this type of relationship.

Practical Marriage Wisdom

CASE STUDY: *My husband is the absolute boss of our home. If I suggested anything to him, he would either yell or lecture me on how it was not my place to tell him what to do. Should I correct him or just let it go? The primary text that I would love for you to help me with is how to restore him in a spirit of gentleness.*

Brothers, if anyone is caught in any transgression, you who are spiritual should restore him in a spirit of gentleness. Keep watch on yourself, lest you too be tempted. Bear one another's burdens, *and so fulfill the law of Christ.*

(Galatians 6:1-2)

There is an aspect of this question that applies to both spouses. At the heart of the issue is one spouse coming alongside another one to provide soul care. In this case study, it's the submitted wife hoping to fulfill the fullest possibilities of a coequal hierarchy. Going and making disciples does not apply only to those who are outside our homes and need to hear the gospel's message (Matthew 28:19-20). Disciple-making is a call for all Christians to care for each other within their spheres of influence, whether inside or outside our homes. Spouses know their mates better than anyone else, and the longer you're married, the more information and insight you have about your spouse. Smart marriage partners want to help each other, which is at the heart of disciple-making. Everyone benefits! To have a person to know you so well and be able to bring wise, loving, and corrective care into your life is sanctification gold. Some spouses do not have this understanding, or perhaps they do, but for inhibiting reasons, they do not bring soul care to each other. My hope for you is that it does not matter if you're a husband or wife but that you can apply these ideas to your marriage.

Dictators Dictate

As for correcting an authoritarian husband, which is what the case study is about, you want to begin with Galatians 6:1-2, as suggested. But there is a significant caveat: if he is an absolute boss husband, he will not listen to your advice or appreciate your care. Only a correctable spouse can be corrected, whether it's a husband or wife. The correctable person is a humble, teachable person who wants to change, and he is appreciative that you speak into his life. The authoritarian husband is a dictator, and those people types do not surround themselves with folks who disagree with them. The wife in a marriage like this is between a rock and a hard place. All of his other friends or relationships will either acquiesce to his domineering personality style or leave the relationship. Authoritarian types surround themselves with people who are not able to challenge the tight-fisted control that they wield.

Correct With Caution

In an ideal world, you should correct your husband when it's needed. Regrettably, this type of spouse does not live in that world. She must be careful about bringing things to his attention. He has a distorted view of submission in the marriage, which makes him the absolute boss, and she's in the role of the subjugated. Rather than seeing himself as a leader who disciples his family, he treats his wife as an unequal entity in the sight of God. Paul's idea of nourishing and cherishing a wife (Ephesians 5:29) is an unknown tongue to this kind of man. He does not have a proper biblical category for strengths and weaknesses or how his spouse could be his most significant asset in their marriage outside of God's friendship and empowering favor (James 4:6). I have dealt with these insecure, unaware, arrogant, domineering authority types many times. It takes an enormous amount of patience, wisdom, courage, kindness, and community to turn them into men who love God and others as much as they love themselves (Matthew 22:36-40; Philippians 2:3-5). I'm not saying it can't happen in this situation, but she must know where the starting line is, which is not his humble cooperativeness, or she may make what could have been avoidable mistakes.

Diagnosing the Dictator

This chapter is not about how to leave or if she should leave her authoritarian husband, which is another type of conversation that requires other questions and counselors. My aim here is to give you insight into a dictator's heart, which will aid you in restoring him in a spirit of gentleness— the question being asked.

- **INSECURE:** The number one problem with a self-reliant person is their vulnerability. A driving motivation for their self-sufficiency is that they are masking their fears and insecurities through outward faux-power. The dictator is a controller, and a controlling person cannot be out of control. They accomplish this illusion by maximizing their strengths while squashing anything or anyone that penetrates their vulnerability force field. They are weaker than you might imagine.

- **UNAWARE:** Because the self-sufficient controller is managing all aspects of his life, there are things he cannot perceive. He's too stubborn and blind to admit that he might be wrong. He's too proud to ask for help. His modus operandi is to maintain an image of authority and power, which means humble admissions of his inadequacy or ignorance are impossible. He presents his carefully edited image to others, which is a manicured, likable reputation that masks his rogue authoritarianism. However, behind the curtain, he's a weak human being.

- **ARROGANT:** His image-making perpetuates the myth of self-importance, which is an elixir that intoxicates him into feeling good about himself. Egotistical self-importance stems from insecurity and fear. He creates a world that he can control, which makes him feel good about himself. He leverages his strengths to attain self-important status, and he permits nobody to bring him down or expose his insecurities, including his wife.

- **BLINDNESS:** If you perpetuate a lie long enough, it will no longer be a lie to you. This person is blind to his blindness, which is the worst possible state of the wayward soul. I trust as you read these things that the Lord will give you pity for a husband like this. For reasons that predate you, there has been a strong desire for him to construct a kingdom where he has always wanted to reign. The blindness of his passion has fully captured his soul.

- **DOMINEERING:** The behavior that you feel and disdain in your husband is his dominance. It's worse as you think about how he is affecting the children. It's at this juncture where a wife senses her most significant tension. On the one hand, she loves (or used to love) her husband, and on the other hand, she is the protective mother who wants to rescue her children.

Gentle Correction

The text the case study referred to is Galatians 6:1-2, and it's because of that text that I'm answering the question the way that I have. The case study does not offer a bailout but how God can use the wife to restore her husband in a spirit of gentleness. There may be another discussion at another time about staying or leaving, but that issue is not in view here. Paul says that the correction of your husband must be in a spirit of gentleness. If you're not doing that, there is something you can change today. Some people take a spirit of gentleness too far. For example, the empathetic restorer will feel sorry for her husband and even blame herself for why he does what he does. The sympathetic restorer will do hard things but not go to the other extreme by using sinful anger, harsh words, or a combative spirit. Sin has captured the husband in this case study. Sadly, most husbands like this don't change unless God breaks them, which you should ask God to do. One of the hard things that I'm implying is you asking the Lord to bring him to a place of brokenness (Luke 15:17). Dismantling is an essential kindness that your husband could receive from the Lord, so asking the Father to do this for you and him would be an act of mercy and courage.

Taking Decisive Action

There are many more things that you must know to help your husband, but in this chapter, I want you to focus on two of them:

- Find your starting point by discerning some of the idolatries in his heart that are motivating him to be as he is. For example, reputation, power, fame, approval, and significance can be some of the idols he worships.
- Guard your heart as you seek those civil moments where you can speak to him, hoping to help him change. One of the most vital things you can do is see him as a prisoner to the chains of his making. You may have to take a different kind of decisive action later, but before you make decisions that are hard to walk back, make sure you're talking to a competent mentor who understands you and your husband and dares to walk you through your marriage crisis. You should not feel any guilt for seeking help outside your marriage. If your husband is an authoritarian, as the case study suggests, then he has disqualified himself from discipling you, and you must submit yourself to your church authority as they guide you through the next steps.

Call to Action

If you're a wife in this situation, be a careful wife who wants to explore all the options, which begins with your primary objective as your husband's redemption—if needed—and then his restoration. You're imitating the gospel in this matter: Christ came to the imprisoned to set them free. Your husband may be set free as you lead him to Jesus. Here are a few thoughts as you explore how to do that.

1. Describe your prayer life, specifically as it relates to your husband. In what ways do you express gratitude for him? What are a few ways in which he is leading well? (Read 1 Corinthians 1:1-9.)

2. Have you crossed the line and are now more of a grumbler, complainer, or gossiper about your husband? If you have transgressed that line, what is your plan for change? Who are you going to enlist to help you change?

3. Talk about what gentle correction looks like in the verse for this case study—Galatians 6:1-2. Would your children characterize you as a person who corrects their daddy with a spirit of gentleness? If not, why not, and what is your plan to change?

4. Are you asking God to break him—to dismantle him?

5. The sympathetic person wants the captured soul to experience freedom. Sometimes, that liberty comes by dramatically breaking the bonds that have bound and incarcerated him. It does not have to happen this way, but it may be what needs to happen. How have your fears hindered you from bringing comprehensive—including courageous—care to him?

6. How have his authoritarian and persuasive
    ways trained you to over-guilt yourself to where
    you believe that his sinfulness is your sin? This
    condition can cloud your thinking, which is why
    you want a sympathetic friend to walk with you
    through this.

8

Something Between Us

The cross of Christ has wonder-working power. It can change you and your relationships, but the process is not a passive "let go and let God" exercise. If Christ's cross is not a practical governing reality in our relationships, we will hurt those we love the most. Though the cross of Christ is not the whole gospel, it's a poignant reminder of the sacrifice needed to sustain a relationship with someone.

Biff and Mable

I was meeting with a couple that had convinced themselves that all the problems in the marriage were the other person's fault. Each spouse was clear about how the other person was sabotaging the marriage. They had their facts straight, and, for the most part, they were correct in their accusations. It did not matter which angle I took. Counseling this couple was futile. They were not going to act like Christians. Both of them had collected just enough information on the other to justify their righteousness as they hurled accusations at each other. Finally, after several attempts to get them to see the fallacy and futility in their positions, I relinquished any further hope of a ceasefire and reconciliation. From my chair, there would be no possible redemptive, relational progress that day. They were too mad, too self-justified, too hurt, too unforgiving, and too stubborn to change. I gave up.

There was nothing else for them to do but double down on their positions. Yep. That is what I told my battling buddies to do. I suggested that they continue their anger toward each other. Keep on keeping on. Duke it out. Since they were determined to bite and devour each other (Galatians 5:15), I appealed to them to keep at it. Then I paused and added, "But under one condition. I want to make a stipulation." I told them that they could fight all they wanted to fight as long as I could choose the location for their Christ-less sparing. Here is how I said it:

> I want you to climb Golgotha's bloody hill, where the multitudes scorned our Savior, as the Father judged Him (Matthew 27:32-44). I want you to go to Calvary, the place where the crucified Son of God became a sin for both of you—the place where the Lord punished Christ for your sins (2 Corinthians 5:21).

Christ took this Christian couple's sins by willingly giving up His life to the scorching judgment of His Father. His sacrifice gave them a free pass, so to speak: God would never judge them for their past, present, and future sins (John 8:36; Romans 8:1). I further appealed to them to position their bodies in such a way that the cross of Christ would be in their virtual sight lines. My hope was for them to get so close to the cross that the blood of the dying Lamb of God could figuratively drop on them as they persisted in their arguments. I added that it would benefit them to intentionally glance at that cross on occasion during their conflict so that while they were wounding each other, they could remember the wounded One, the person who took their transgressions (Isaiah 53:5).

I hoped that the wooden beam (Matthew 7:3-5) would

become an impediment to their blows—that they would have to stretch around the cross before the other person could experience the intended marital pain. I wanted the cross to always be in their view, particularly when their anger toward each other escalated. As things stood, the cross was not preeminent in their thinking. Christ, at best, was on the periphery of their lives as they persisted in their argumentation. When the cross is more about a necklace than a sacrifice, we have the wrong cross in view. I wanted them to experience the historical fact of the dying Lamb of God visually and viscerally. I hoped God's Spirit would burn the revelations about the gospel deep into their minds. I wanted them to be affected by the horrible realities of the cross of Christ.

Are You Dying Today?

Perhaps you are tempted to sinful anger at your spouse, children, friends, or enemies. How does the cross of Christ influence your arguments?

- Does the cross of Christ change your frustration toward others?
- How easy (or difficult) is it for you to know the truths of the cross while holding on to unforgiveness?
- Does the cross steer you from judgmental, condemning thoughts toward those who have offended you?

One of the most practical ways to reconcile with those who have hurt you is through the cross of Christ.

- How could we treat others in such a way that God would not treat us, as we consider that He has already meted punishment on His one and only Son for the sins that we have committed (John 3:16)?

- How could we hold judgment toward or hurt others when Christ refuses to hold judgment against or punish us? If the cross of Christ is not our motive for humble forgiveness, we will be like this battling couple.
- What is your motivation for forgiveness, whether it is attitudinal (Luke 23:34) or transactional (Matthew 6:14-15)? Is it the cross of Christ? A proper motive for forgiveness comes from a right understanding of Christ's work on the cross.

Let all bitterness and wrath and anger and clamor and slander be put away from you, along with all malice. Be kind to one another, tenderhearted, forgiving one another, as God in Christ forgave you.
(Ephesians 4:31-32)

Call to Action

1. What was Paul's motive for letting all bitterness, wrath, and anger go?
2. What was his reason for forgiveness, kindness, and tenderheartedness toward another person? The answer is in this statement: "...as God in Christ forgave you." Paul tied his motive for a right attitude toward others to the cross of Christ. Your motivation to forgive is because God has forgiven you.
3. If you are not a Christian, the first place to experience forgiveness is to ask God to forgive you, and He will adopt you into His family.
4. If you are a Christian, but the cross is not in your sight lines as you think about others, I appeal to you to work through the questions in this chapter.

9

Practical Help for Restoration

Some husbands and wives can have a hard time putting a broken marriage back together. Typically, expectations and disappointments create a backlog of unresolved conflict. Unforgiveness sets in, the death toll to any relationship. When a couple gets to this point, pride becomes the unscaleable wall between them. They have lost the vision of Christ and His church in their union. I've developed this reflective study to help a couple in this situation to tear down that seemingly insurmountable wall.

A Couple's Warning

The worst way to read this chapter is with the word "but" at the tip of your tongue. I'm speaking of excuse-making here. If your initial reaction to anything I say points first to your spouse, you could be beyond help. Jesus talked about log assessment before any speck considerations in Matthew 7:3-5. If you don't do it His way, you won't find the help you desire. Secondly, you have to read this chapter without mapping your experience over the situation. I realize none of us are purely objective. On our most objective days, our experiences will still influence us, detaching us from the richness and purity of God's Word.

You must fight to be biblical and not elevate your experience above God's Word. It may serve you well to share this chapter with a courageous friend who is not afraid to speak the truth to you. Finally, before you go further, ask the Spirit of God to help you with these two things.

- Tell Him that it's your desire not to make excuses.
- Ask Him to help you not to be experience-centered.

Your goal is to be open, honest, vulnerable, and willing to change, no matter how hard it may seem initially. Broken marriages require triage; there is no other way. What I'm asking you to do is impossibly hard, which is why you need the Lord's empowering favor and guidance.

A Wife's Role

The wife is analogous to the church in marriage. She has the opportunity to model the church practically to her husband. While it is true that the church reflects the Savior's leading, loving, and sacrificing, it is also true that the church should humbly respond to His leadership. "But my husband does not lead!" This retort is a sad reality in too many marriages. In such cases, the wife still has an obligation and opportunity to demonstrate humility and love toward her husband (1 Peter 3:1-6; Ephesians 5:22, 23). She can love her husband in a similar gospel-centered manner in which the Lord loves her: when she is not responsive to or meritorious of His love (Romans 5:8; Ephesians 2:8-9). To love only the lovable is where the culture places the bar in a relationship. Christian spouses must do better than that.

If you love those who love you, what benefit is that to you? For even sinners love those who love them. And if you do good to those who do good to you, what benefit is that to you? For even sinners do the same.
(Luke 6:32-33)

A Wife's Self-Assessment

- Are you waiting for your husband to change before you love him biblically, or do you love him even though he is not leading well—at this time?
- If you do not biblically love him, would you consider how that attitude is counter to the gospel? Please explain.
- Are you aware that loving him well includes bringing discipleship care to him, which could mean you are correcting him or going over his authoritative head to access the help you need in the marriage? Please explain.
- Do you realize the vital role you play in your marriage as you humbly allow God to work through you to help your husband mature? Please explain.

A Husband's Role

"Husbands, love your wives, as Christ loved the church." What a beautiful picture. It's a template for you to imitate. The prototype for what all relationships should look like in a marriage covenant. It's the clearest and most profound picture for husbands and wives to emulate. The husband is the representative or a picture of Christ in the marriage. Analogously, he is Christ. Isn't that helpful? Dear husband, have you ever wondered how you are going to behave in your marriage? Doesn't a picture of Christ clear it up for you? You are a picture of Christ to your wife. All you have to do is imitate Him. What would Jesus do? Doesn't that give a new meaning to the overused WWJD marketing cliche from the late twentieth century? Paul gets right to the point. In nine words, he gives you the most precise and comprehensive job description you need to be a rock star husband.

Husbands, love your wives, as Christ loved the church and gave himself up for her (Ephesians 5:25).

A Husband's Self-Assessment

- In what areas are you appropriating the grace of God in your marriage? What is working well for you?
- How are you imitating Christ to your wife?
- Ask your wife for her assessment regarding your imitation of Christ. Does she see similar things?
- If your children are older, ask them for their perspective on your replication of Christ. This time of collaborative reflection and assessment could be a wonderful time of encouragement as well as opportunities to grow as a husband.
- What are a couple of ways you need to change to bring a clearer picture of Jesus Christ to your marriage? Will you let your spouse know where you need to change and solicit her help?
- Will you both work together on maintaining your Christ and church-emulating strategy?

A Damaged Picture

It is a challenge for many couples to model Christ (husband) or the church (wife) in their marriages because of their ongoing struggle with sin. They like the idea of what the imitation of Christ and His church could be in their marriage, but they struggle with the process that leads to that beautiful picture. Some couples do not carefully consider the respective fallen natures that they brought into the relationship. Perhaps the questions in this chapter will help both of you as you talk about your marriage. Discussing them could open the door for you to experience the Lord working in your relationship. God gives grace to the humble (James 4:6). Husband, humbly lead your wife through this chapter. Wife, will you humbly put on a respectful and loving picture of the church? May you both expect and experience new depths of the grace of God.

Call to Action

1. Encourage your spouse by identifying how you have seen God's grace actively working in their life.
2. Discuss some ways you could change to serve your spouse more effectively.
3. What are the benefits of being other-centered instead of thinking about what your spouse can do for you?
4. Pray together, thanking the Lord for the privilege of cooperating with Him in sanctifying each other.
5. Discuss how praying together creates a healthy vulnerability between you.

Conclusion

Marriage counseling has historically been the most common type of counseling I have done, which makes sense because the marriage relationship is unique in that there is not supposed to be an escape clause. Marriage is for life. This fact makes marriage the perfect context for relationship sharpening. There are times when counseling is essential because of the fallenness of the couple and the need for community. If your marriage is bad, you more than likely are doing some of the following things. These are some of the most oft-repeated mistakes I have seen in poor marriages. I have written them satirically. A gentleman read this list a few years ago and wrote to me saying that he had committed all of these things in his former marriage. He wrote me in tears. This list is in no particular order. If any of these bad practices characterize your marriage, be hopeful: I have ten tips that can help you have a wonderful marriage at the end. I have also added some helpful diagnostic questions in the final section to help you and your spouse become the couple you desire to be.

TIP #1: ALWAYS HAVE THE LAST WORD
I know James talked about being quick to listen and slow to speak, but if you want to win your sparring match with your spouse, you must have the last word (James 1:19). One of the most effective ways to accomplish this is to not listen

to your spouse. What you do while she is talking is start formulating what you want to say next. You let her wax on while you're figuring out how to outmaneuver her droning. If she likes to talk a lot and if you're a little slow on the uptake, you will have more time to come back at her once she stops chattering.

TIP #2: GET HER WITH A CHEAP SHOT
Corrupting speech, like criticism and sarcasm, is effective here. This sin habit is counter to Paul's appeal in Ephesians 4:29 to build up the other person with your words, but we're talking about winning. Don't let humility or gospel-centered posturing get in the way here. Sarcasm literally means to cut the flesh. It's like a meat cutter who cuts away non-valued parts. When you use sarcasm on your spouse, it's a way to devalue her. No doubt this will put her in her place as you get a leg up on the marriage communication competition.

TIP #3: TWIST HER WORDS TO TIE HER UP
This tip is for the more advanced competitor. Twisting up your wife requires a certain amount of mental agility, but if she is truly the weaker vessel and you're any man at all, you should be able to win this battle of words, too. One of the keys here is to harden your conscience (Hebrews 3:7-8). Perchance, the Spirit of God tries to illuminate or convince you to change, you can go into rationalization or excuse mode. This reaction to the Spirit will effectively mute your inner voice (Romans 2:14-15). A little self-deception goes a long way.

TIP #4: PUSH THE "IT'S NOT MY JOB" WORLDVIEW
A man's work is outside the home, and a woman's job is inside the home. Make this Scripture-twisting agenda your own by being the comatose husband while at home. Grab the remote and surf the 900+ channels, or bury yourself in

the Internet. You can also guilt-trip her by making a few well-placed criticisms about how she keeps the house. The home is your castle, and she's the keeper of it. Most women want to please their husbands, so if you keep the carrot dangled in front of her, she will always be trying hard to please you.

TIP #5: NEVER BE WRONG

Admitting your mistakes is a weakness. Though John wants you to confess your sins (1 John 1:7-10), the proud man never has sins to confess. This posture will require more self-deception on your part, but if you have any game at all, you can pull this off (Hebrews 4:7). Justification is your best friend. To justify is to declare yourself not guilty. Of course, you know only the Lord can justify you, but we're talking about winning, right? If you continually declare yourself not guilty, your wife will soon get the message and give up trying to convince you of anything. You will win, and she will be sufficiently defeated.

Okay, ladies. Here are a few tips to get the ball rolling on your side. With a little practice, you could be a primary source of discouragement to your husband. By the way, the previous five tips can work for you, too.

TIP #6: WITHHOLD ENCOURAGEMENT

Paul talked about how kindness is the ingredient the Lord uses to motivate a person to change (Romans 2:4). To be kind is to build up. It's a way to motivate by grace. Always looking for evidence of God's kindness in your husband is what I'm talking about. Don't do that. If you withhold encouragement, he will become demoralized. This attitude is what I call the "whupped pup" syndrome. If you're not kind to him, he will begin to shut down. Your once strong and confident guy will fold like cheap laundry.

TIP #7: NAG HIM TO DEATH

The last tip was about withholding something. This tip is about giving him something. Become the dripping faucet Solomon talked about in Proverbs 27:15. Your critical words will be like little sharp daggers in his heart—death by a thousand paper cuts. Eventually, he will give up. To withhold encouragement while being critical of him is the perfect one-two punch that will end in a knockout every time. You will quickly have him waving the white flag—unless he starts seeking encouragement from someone else.

TIP #8: BE OVER-SENSITIVE

The key to this tip is to put him on eggshells, a counterintuitive move: The way to win is to be weak. It's kind of like the Bible (2 Corinthians 4:7). But if you pervert the fragile vase Peter talked about (1 Peter 3:7) by being emotional and irrational, he may acquiesce and give up on the marriage. You will have him so paranoid that he'll be afraid to say or do anything. Keep him guessing with your emotional rollercoaster. He'll never know how you will respond. At that point, you will own him.

TIP #9: OVER-COMMIT SO YOU'RE ALWAYS TIRED

Over-scheduling your life will kill any marriage. Your goal is to always be on the go. Be busy during the day and tired at night. This lifestyle will motivate him to find other things to do. Just pray the other things are not another woman or porn. If you have children, this will be easy for you. Get them signed up for as many extra-curricular activities as possible. Kill marriage time and crank up the van. Worship the sports gods. The key here is to be busy and tired.

TIP #10: BRING UP PAST WRONGS

Never let go of the past. You will not have to worry about his current blunders if you keep parading his past in front of him. If you both had sex before marriage, for example, it's a done deal. He will never be able to overcome that mistake. God has wired him to be a leader. The more you remind him of his failures, the more you will be able to eviscerate what the Lord has put into him. Eventually, he will lose heart and accept your assessment: he is a loser.

Thoughts On Losing

Jesus was a loser, according to many people. Even His closest friends were tripped up by His leadership style (Mark 8:32). It got so bad that at the end of His life, they all left Him (Matthew 26:56). They could not accept losing as the path to winning. After all His teaching, they still did not understand the backwardness of the gospel (1 Corinthians 1:18-25).

But many who are first will be last, and the last first (Matthew 19:30). So the last will be first, and the first last (Matthew 20:16). They did not want to be last, and they did not want to lose. They were like us: winning was all that mattered, even if someone had to cut off a person's ear to secure the victory (John 18:10). To grab a towel and basin of water was beneath them (John 13:1-17). To give their life in exchange for someone else was a bridge too far for their selfish minds to grasp (John 15:13; Mark 10:45; Ephesians 5:25). They were myopic in their vision of God's plan for others (Hebrews 12:2). Winning was winning and losing was losing, but from a Christian worldview, losing is winning.

If you can't embrace losing, as in being second in your marriage, you will be the biggest loser of all (Ephesians 5:12). Not only will you go down swinging, but you will take your marriage down with you. To win at all costs creates an unbiblical competition between two people. This spirit of competitiveness can be at its most acute within the marriage covenant. When a couple becomes more like competitors, the marriage is lost. When winning or losing are the most important things in the relationship, the marriage is fast-tracking toward dysfunction. If any of the ten previous tips describe you, I appeal for you to change. You will not win at marriage or any other relationship if you refuse to humble yourself by taking on the counterintuitive life of Jesus. This warning is why I'm leaving you with ten positive tips, plus a few assessment questions to discuss with your spouse. If you can't discuss these things without getting into an argument, please find help now.

Tip #1: Seek to Listen, Not Speak

1. How actively do you listen?
2. Is your goal to help your spouse be clear or get your points made? Please explain.
3. Do you know how to draw out your spouse so they can be a more effective communicator?

Tip #2: Uplift With Your Words

1. Would your spouse characterize you as an encourager? Why or why not?
2. Do you actively seek to find ways to say "thank you" to your spouse?
3. Are you regularly thanking God for your spouse? If not, why not?

Tip #3: Give Her Space and Grace to Speak

1. Do you create contexts of grace that free your spouse to express all her thoughts?
2. Do you give your spouse room to make communication mistakes because it's not about saying it perfectly? It's about understanding each other.
3. Are you regularly thinking about your spouse, seeking to understand her more effectively? What does that look like in your marriage?

TIP #4: YOUR JOB CONTINUES AFTER YOU ARRIVE HOME

1. Do you proactively plan time with your spouse?
2. Are you regularly asking your spouse how you can be a more effective servant?
3. How do you need to change in these areas?

TIP #5: YOU ARE NOT ENTIRELY SANCTIFIED

1. Do you have a biblical self-suspicion about yourself?
2. Are you quicker to admit your wrongs than your spouse's wrongs? Please explain.
3. What is it about you that makes it hard to confess your sins to your spouse?

TIP #6: THE KINDNESS OF GOD LEADS TO CHANGE

1. Is it impossible for you to keep from saying kind things to your spouse?
2. What does your spouse receive the most from you: your displeasure or your encouragement?
3. What needs to change regarding your spousal communication?

TIP #7: CONTENTMENT IS A BEAUTIFUL JEWEL

1. How does your spouse experience your discontentment? How do you need to change?
2. Do you regularly identify your grumbling and biblically repent of it? If not, why not?
3. In what ways has your spouse become an idol?

TIP #8: GOD IS YOUR STRENGTH

1. How does the grace of God help you take every thought captive? See 2 Corinthians 10:3-6.
2. In what ways are you over-sensitive, and how does that speak to the idols of your heart?
3. What do you fear regarding your marriage, or what are you afraid of in your marriage?

Tip #9: Calendar Planning Is a Stewardship Issue

1. How do you need to change your calendar to change your marriage?
2. Does your spouse get your best time or your leftover time?
3. How do you both need to change to make each other a calendar time priority?

Tip #10: The Gospel Neutralizes All Sin

1. Are there past sins you both have not resolved? If not, why not?
2. If past sins are neutralized by and delivered to God, do you still bring them up for marital review in a punitive way? Why?
3. How does your self-righteousness play out in your marriage? Self-righteousness is a greater than/ better than attitude.

Please talk to your spouse about these things. If that is impossible at this time, will you appeal to your local church leaders to help you with your marriage?

About the Author

 Rick Thomas launched the Life Over Coffee global training network in 2008 to bring hope and help for you and others by creating resources that spark conversations for transformation. His primary responsibilities are resource creation and leadership development, which he does through speaking, writing, podcasting, and educating. In 1990 he earned a BA in Theology and, in 1991, a BS in Education. In 1993, he received his ordination into Christian ministry, and in 2000, he graduated with an MA in Counseling from The Master's University. In 2006, he was recognized as a Fellow of the Association of Certified Biblical Counselors (ACBC).

Other Books Available from
Life Over Coffee

Boasting in Weakness
Centering Your Marriage on Christ
Communication
Complete Marriage
Don't Apologize
Exchange the Truth for a Lie
Help My Marriage Has Grown Cold
Identity Crisis
Local Church
Loving Me
Mad
Marriage Devotion We Are One
Politics and Culture
Parenting Devotion from Zero to Adulthood
Sex, Temptation, and Modesty
Storm Hurler
The Cyber Effect
The Talk
Wives Leading
You Decide

www.ingramcontent.com/pod-product-compliance
Lightning Source LLC
Chambersburg PA
CBHW071534120626
46550CB00006B/2463